CONTENTS

COPYRIGHT NOTICE

FIRST THINGS FIRST

Before you get started it's important to note that this is a workbook, i.e. I don't just talk at you, I have you doing exercises and answering questions so, if you bought this book on Kindle you have two choices:

You can either read the questions on your Kindle (or Kindle app) and answer the questions on separate pieces of paper which could get a bit messy and complicated when filling in the tables, OR (highly recommended) download a free PDF from my website which you can either type into on your computer as it's editable, or you can go old school and print it off and write your answers in pen.

Click here to get your free download.
If you can't click the link, please go to: http://lisacherrybeaumont.com/lpa-download

INTRODUCTION

Hello lovely! Welcome to Life Purpose Alchemy, I'm so delighted that you're here.

THANK YOU for committing to finding out what you're meant to be doing at this stage in your life, and for getting on with it! You're a rare breed and I salute you.

I understand what it's like to be stuck in a job that's just not quite doing it for you or hopping from one unfulfilling business to the next. You're going through the motions but, well, you KNOW there's something else that you're destined for!

Well, there's no need for you to be stuck like I was, going round in circles for years, trying to figure it out. By the end, you will have not only a clear understanding of your purpose, but also a set of action steps to get you started.

Hello, by the way, I'm Lisa Cherry Beaumont, The Life Purpose Alchemist, and I'm here to help you find out what you love and go do it for a living. My style of coaching works on the premise that YOU have all your own answers inside of you, and it's my job to get them out.

You will be guided through questions to help you identify specifically what you want your life to look like, what your purpose is at this stage in your life, what your own personal values are, and then help you to combine them to create your ideal work. I'll get you over the ten most common fears when it comes to going after your dream work, and then you'll set your dream work as a goal and create tangible steps to get you started.

Some of the questions may seem repetitive but that's for good reason – to help you really dig deep – so just go with it. And some of the questions may seem irrelevant to you so, although it's better to answer all of the questions if you can, if something really doesn't make sense to you, it's OK to skip it and move on to the next. There are no right or wrong answers, but I have offered examples here and there to help you understand some of the questions.

And there is no right or wrong way to work through this book. You can go through all the exercises in the same day, from start to finish. Or you can work on one step at a time, steadily, day by day. Or you can treat it as a live, working document that you return to again and again, as you spend time digesting the results of each exercise and gaining further clarity, popping back to check what's still resonating with you, over time. There's enormous value in each of these methods and you can do what feels right to you. The main thing is for you to keep going.

OK, ready to live your purpose? Let's get started!

STEP 1: YOUR DREAM LIFESTYLE

WELCOME TO Step 1 of Life Purpose Alchemy.

Statistics state that the average person (and I know you're not the average person!) spends more time planning their annual holiday than they do planning their future.

And I'll add to that, even those who commit to a New Year's Resolution often aren't thinking about their dreams or their bigger picture.

In order to get what we want, it's essential to define, decide and design exactly what we want, otherwise how are we going to work towards or it even recognise it if and when we get there?

There's an old song from the early '80s that goes, "You've got to have a dream, if you don't have a dream, how're you gonna have a dream come true?" And I agree, wholeheartedly.

So let's start thinking about *your* dream life. Here's some questions to get you started. Write whatever comes to mind and don't let your limiting beliefs get in the way. I won't allow, "I'd love that but..." Write it down! Where there's a will there's a way.

Let's start by looking at your identity:

1. What five things do you like most about yourself? (Don't over-think it, just spit out whatever comes to mind.)

1

2

3

4

5

2. What four things do other people say you're really good at?

1

2

3

4

3. What three things do you enjoy doing the most?

1

2

3

4. What two things would you do if you had 50 million dollars in the bank and all the time in the world?

1

2

5. What one thing must you have done by the time you're 100 years old?

1

Now let's look at how you'd like your dream life to look:

6. Describe your perfect day from when you get up to when you go to bed.

7. When your life is ideal, what kind of people will you spend time with?

8. What will you do for enjoyment?

9. How will you feel in your ideal life?

10. What skills do you have to help you create your ideal life?

11. Who can help you on this journey?

Well done! Designing your dream lifestyle is THAT SIMPLE. This gives a broad overview of what you're about and is a terrific starting point for discovering your life purpose which is what we'll be finding out in Step 2.

STEP 2: YOUR LIFE PURPOSE

Welcome to Step 2 of Life Purpose Alchemy.

We've all got things we lose ourselves in when we do them and, no matter what our limiting beliefs are about earning money doing it, I 99% guarantee you can turn whatever it is into your livelihood.

You may already consciously know what it is – and if you do, lucky you! Do this exercise anyway, as it's good for you to explore your strengths and it may remind you of a passion that you'd forgotten all about under the avalanche of daily life.

You don't have to have an Olympic medal in whatever-it-is, just keep an open mind, don't edit what you write, just get some ideas flowing.

It's normal during this step to feel some resistance to the questions. If that happens, and you find yourself fretting that you can't think of anything, DON'T PANIIIIIIIC!!!!!!! No, seriously, don't worry, just have a quick read through the questions and then take a break and come back to it when you're ready.

12. What do you find yourself doing on holidays or days off that you enjoy?

13. What activities make you lose track of time?

14. Imagine you came into a life-changing sum of money today. What would you find yourself doing in two years' time?

15. What events and activities do you really look forward to?

16. And what is it about these events/activities that you look forward to?

17. What are you really good at?

18. What do you do well that surprises people?

19. What activities make your heart sing and/or give you that warm, fuzzy feeling of a job well done?

20. If you secretly knew what you were put on this planet to do, what would that be? If you don't know, imagine if you *did* know; what would it be?

21. What have you not mentioned already that needs to be included?

22. If you knew you absolutely could not fail, what is it you would do with your life?

23. From all of the above, whittle it down to three things you'd love to get paid to do.

1

2

3

Notes:

24. If you had to choose two of those three, which would they be?

1

2

Notes:

25. Even if you have no idea how you could possibly get paid to do it, choose the one that you know in your heart is what you'd dearly love to do.

1

Notes:

26. If you seriously struggled to choose one of your options from question 23, try combining them. Come up with at least three different ways you can combine them:

1.

2.

3.

You're not alone if, at this stage, you have a vague answer like "help people".

We all want to help people – like someone once said, "we're all just walking each other home" – but it's the HOW you help people that's important, so if "help people" is your answer, think about your strengths around how you currently help people. There's no room for vague, you need to be specific. For example:

I'm a coach and I help people to live their purpose.

Some build houses and that helps to give people homes.

Others grow food that helps people to eat healthily.

So look back at all your answers and think about what you're *already doing* that helps people, either directly or indirectly, whether you're currently getting paid for it or not.

27. I help people by:

28. I want to help people by:

Using what you've written for questions 25, 26, 27, 28 (or a combination) complete this sentence:

Even though I may not yet be considered an expert, and even though I may not yet be able to see how I can make a living from this, I realise that, at this moment in time...

29. I am on this planet to:

... and this is my purpose.

Well, would you look at that! GO YOU! What a superstar. I'm so proud of you. In the next step, we're going to delve into your personal values. (The next step is my personal favourite and will give you the most useful information anyone has ever told you about yourself. I'm not exaggerating.)

LisaCherryBeaumont.com

STEP 3: YOUR DEALBREAKERS & FEELGOODS

Welcome to Step 3 of Life Purpose Alchemy.

In this step you're going to work out your own personal values. This information will tell you specifically what your driving forces are behind the things that you do, and what makes you feel good.

In a nutshell, this exercise will tell you what needs to be in place in your work so that you will enjoy it, and what needs to be in place that will make you stick at it. And also, just as importantly, what factors will make you quit!

It's quite an involved process but you mustn't skip it! Stick with it because the information is truly valuable and you'll need it in a later step. It's not difficult, but you do need to focus, so give yourself about an hour.

As with the previous steps, don't overthink your answers, go with what comes to you quickly.

When I say "employment" I'm talking about paid work, volunteer work, your own business, and voluntary training courses.

You have space to record 8 of your most recent "employments". If you haven't had as many as 8, fill in as many as you've had. It doesn't matter if you were there for two days or twenty years, you must record it. It doesn't matter if it was poorly paid, unpaid, or just one morning a week, you must use it as it'll give you important information.

You're going to start with your most recent employment, and work backwards.

I'll give you real-life examples of my own so you can see how it works.

I feckin' love this exercise. I'm excited for you!

Real-life example:

Job Title *Office Manager*

What made you start this employment (/job/business/course)?
What were those factors that made you decide this is what you needed at that moment in time?

The work would be varied	I'd be working with smart people	The offices were beautiful	It was good money

What made you leave this employment (job/business/course)?
If it was the end of a fixed contract, or the end of the course, or you were made redundant, if you'd had the chance to continue further, would you have? If YES, skip this question. If no, you'd have left anyway, what was it that would have made you leave?

The work began to feel pointless	It became monotonous; I wasn't learning anything new	I wasn't using my unique skills; I felt like anyone could do it	I wanted to travel

What did you enjoy most about it?
Even if the good feelings weren't there all the time, or they didn't last, when you DID feel happy, joyous or extremely satisfied in this employment (/job/business/course) what contributed to that feeling?

Varied tasks, lots of different aspects to the job	I got to do lots of organising and making things more efficient
I was trusted to do things my way and left to get on with it	I was able to be visually creative with design of business cards and letterheads, etc.
I had a great computer and fantastic internet which made my job smooth and effortless	I got excellent feedback and the work I did was very much appreciated because I was good at it

Your most recent employment (job/business/course):

Job Title

What made you start this employment (/job/business/course)?
What were those factors that made you decide this is what you needed at that moment in time?

What made you leave this employment (job/business/course)?
If it was the end of a fixed contract, or the end of the course, or you were made redundant, if you'd had the chance to continue further, would you have? If YES, skip this question. If no, you'd have left anyway, what was it that would have made you leave?

What did you enjoy most about it?
Even if the good feelings weren't there all the time, or they didn't last, when you DID feel happy, joyous or extremely satisfied in this employment (/job/business/course) what contributed to that feeling?

Your next most recent employment (job/business/course):

Job Title

What made you start this employment (/job/business/course)?
What were those factors that made you decide this is what you needed at that moment in time?

What made you leave this employment (job/business/course)?
If it was the end of a fixed contract, or the end of the course, or you were made redundant, if you'd had the chance to continue further, would you have? If YES, skip this question. If no, you'd have left anyway, what was it that would have made you leave?

What did you enjoy most about it?
Even if the good feelings weren't there all the time, or they didn't last, when you DID feel happy, joyous or extremely satisfied in this employment (/job/business/course) what contributed to that feeling?

Your next most recent employment (job/business/course):

Job Title

What made you start this employment (/job/business/course)?
What were those factors that made you decide this is what you needed at that moment in time?

What made you leave this employment (job/business/course)?
If it was the end of a fixed contract, or the end of the course, or you were made redundant, if you'd had the chance to continue further, would you have? If YES, skip this question. If no, you'd have left anyway, what was it that would have made you leave?

What did you enjoy most about it?
Even if the good feelings weren't there all the time, or they didn't last, when you DID feel happy, joyous or extremely satisfied in this employment (/job/business/course) what contributed to that feeling?

Your next most recent employment (job/business/course):

Job Title

What made you start this employment (/job/business/course)?
What were those factors that made you decide this is what you needed at that moment in time?

What made you leave this employment (job/business/course)?
If it was the end of a fixed contract, or the end of the course, or you were made redundant, if you'd had the chance to continue further, would you have? If YES, skip this question. If no, you'd have left anyway, what was it that would have made you leave?

What did you enjoy most about it?
Even if the good feelings weren't there all the time, or they didn't last, when you DID feel happy, joyous or extremely satisfied in this employment (/job/business/course) what contributed to that feeling?

Your next most recent employment (job/business/course):

Job Title

What made you start this employment (/job/business/course)?
What were those factors that made you decide this is what you needed at that moment in time?

What made you leave this employment (job/business/course)?
If it was the end of a fixed contract, or the end of the course, or you were made redundant, if you'd had the chance to continue further, would you have? If YES, skip this question. If no, you'd have left anyway, what was it that would have made you leave?

What did you enjoy most about it?
Even if the good feelings weren't there all the time, or they didn't last, when you DID feel happy, joyous or extremely satisfied in this employment (/job/business/course) what contributed to that feeling?

Your next most recent employment (job/business/course):

Job Title

What made you start this employment (/job/business/course)?
What were those factors that made you decide this is what you needed at that moment in time?

What made you leave this employment (job/business/course)?
If it was the end of a fixed contract, or the end of the course, or you were made redundant, if you'd had the chance to continue further, would you have? If YES, skip this question. If no, you'd have left anyway, what was it that would have made you leave?

What did you enjoy most about it?
Even if the good feelings weren't there all the time, or they didn't last, when you DID feel happy, joyous or extremely satisfied in this employment (/job/business/course) what contributed to that feeling?

Your next most recent employment (job/business/course):

Job Title

What made you start this employment (/job/business/course)?
What were those factors that made you decide this is what you needed at that moment in time?

What made you leave this employment (job/business/course)?
If it was the end of a fixed contract, or the end of the course, or you were made redundant, if you'd had the chance to continue further, would you have? If YES, skip this question. If no, you'd have left anyway, what was it that would have made you leave?

What did you enjoy most about it?
Even if the good feelings weren't there all the time, or they didn't last, when you DID feel happy, joyous or extremely satisfied in this employment (/job/business/course) what contributed to that feeling?

Your next most recent employment (job/business/course):

Job Title

What made you start this employment (/job/business/course)?
What were those factors that made you decide this is what you needed at that moment in time?

What made you leave this employment (job/business/course)?
If it was the end of a fixed contract, or the end of the course, or you were made redundant, if you'd had the chance to continue further, would you have? If YES, skip this question. If no, you'd have left anyway, what was it that would have made you leave?

What did you enjoy most about it?
Even if the good feelings weren't there all the time, or they didn't last, when you DID feel happy, joyous or extremely satisfied in this employment (/job/business/course) what contributed to that feeling?

Well done! Now you're going to take all this information and start to refine it. You're looking for repeaters, i.e. words or phrases that you've used more than once, OR words or phrases that basically mean the same thing.

For example, as an Office Manager one of the reasons I took the job was that "the offices were beautiful". As a Hotel Conference Organiser one of the reasons I took the job was that it was in a "visually nice environment". For me, these amount to the same thing, i.e. one of the factors that drew me to each of these jobs was that I liked the look of the office surroundings.

Input the words or phrase from these exercises, one at a time, into the table on page 27 and, at the same time, look out carefully for repeaters.

When you come to a word or phrase that you've already used (or one that means the same thing), instead of writing it into a new box, put a mark in the box next to where you've already used it, which indicates that you've used it more than once.

Use my examples on the following three pages as a guide.

You do exactly the same thing for each of the questions:

There are three separate columns, one each for your answers to the questions:

"What made you start this employment?"

"What made you leave this employment?"

"What did you enjoy most about it?"

     LisaCherryBeaumont.com

Real-life examples:

Job Title *Office Manager*

What made you start this employment (/job/business/course)?

The work would be varied	I'd be working with smart people	The offices were beautiful	It was good money

Job Title Hotel Conference Organiser

What made you start this employment (/job/business/course)?

Enjoy the work because it's lots of mixed tasks	Interactive, i.e. I don't have to work alone	Visually nice environment to work in	More money

Job Title Graphic Designer

What made you start this employment (/job/business/course)?

Always wanted to do it – dream come true	I enjoy visual design	Learning something new	(No other reasons)

	DEALBREAKERS		FEELGOODS	
What made you start?		What made you leave?	What did you enjoy most?	
Work would be varied	1			
Working with smart people				
Offices were beautiful	1			
Good money	1			
Interactive, not working alone				
Always wanted to do it, dream come true				
Enjoy visual design				
Learn something new				

Job Title *Office Manager*

What made you leave this employment (job/business/course)?

The work began to feel pointless	It became monotonous; not learning anything new	I wasn't using my unique skills; anyone could do it	I wanted to travel

Job Title Hotel Conference Organiser

What made you leave this employment (job/business/course)?

Wanted to go and live in London	(No other reasons)		

Job Title Graphic Designer

What made you leave this employment (job/business/course)?

Offered money to take voluntary redudancy	It was very lonely work	I wanted to travel	I was bored

DEALBREAKERS					FEELGOODS	
What made you start?		What made you leave?			What did you enjoy most?	
Work would be varied	1	Work began to feel pointless				
Working with smart people		Monotonous, not learning anything new	1			
Offices were beautiful	1	Not using my unique skills, anyone could do it				
Good money	1	Wanted to travel	1	1		
Interactive, not working alone		Offered money to take voluntary redundancy				
Always wanted to do it, dream come true		It was very lonely work				
Enjoy visual design						
Learn something new						

LisaCherryBeaumont.com

Job Title *Office Manager* What did you enjoy most about it?

Varied tasks, lots of different aspects to the job	Lots of organising and making things work efficiently
I was trusted to do things my way and left to get on with it	Designing business cards and letterheads, etc.
Great computer and fantastic internet = smooth working!	I got excellent feedback and my work was appreciated

Job Title *Hotel Conference Organiser* What did you enjoy most about it?

Organising! Making sense of clients' needs & making them happen	Interaction with other people, and being part of a team
Autonomy (left to get on with it and do it my way)	Designing Christmas leaflets and restaurant menus
When I got thank you letters from happy clients	(Nothing else)

Job Title *Graphic Designer* What did you enjoy most about it?

Autonomy	Using design and colour and images
Learning new skills	Working with smart people
Translating an idea into a finished product	(Nothing else)

DEALBREAKERS				FEELGOODS	
What made you start?		What made you leave?		What did you enjoy most?	
Work would be varied	1	Work began to feel pointless		Varied tasks	
Working with smart people		Monotonous, not learning anything new	1	Trusted to do it my way & get on with it	1 1
Offices were beautiful	1	Not using my unique skills, anyone could do it		Great computer & internet	
Good money	1	Wanted to travel	1 1	Organising, making things efficient	1 1
Interactive, not working alone		Offered money to take voluntary redundancy		Designing business cards, letterheads...	1 1
Always wanted to do it, dream come true		It was very lonely work		Excellent feedback and appreciation	1
Enjoy visual design				Interaction with others, part of team	
Learn something new				Learning new skills	
				Working with smart people	

 LisaCherryBeaumont.com

30. Input your answers from the forms you just filled in, looking out for and taking note of repeaters.

DEALBREAKERS		FEELGOODS
What made you start?	What made you leave?	What did you enjoy most?

LisaCherryBeaumont.com

You will end up with 3 columns of information that will look a lot like this:

DEALBREAKERS				FEELGOODS	
What made you start?		What made you leave?		What did you enjoy most?	
Work would be varied	① ①	Work began to feel pointless		Varied tasks	1
Working with smart people	1	Monotonous, not learning anything new	① ① ①	Trusted to do things my way and get on with it	① ① ① ①
Offices were beautiful	① ① ①	Not using my unique skills, anyone could do it	1	Great computer & internet	
Good money	① ① ①	Wanted to travel	① ①	Organising, making things work efficiently	① ① ① ①
Interactive, not working alone	1	Money	① ① ①	Designing business cards, letterheads, etc.	① ① ①
Always wanted to do it, dream come true		It was very lonely work	① ①	Excellent feedback and appreciation	① ①
Enjoy visual design		To do something more creative		Interaction with others, being part of a team	
Learn something new		Shitty offices		Learning new skills	
Organising	1			Working with smart people	
I could do the work easily	1			I was good at it	
Allowed me to move to London					
Using my unique talents					
Felt like it would be fulfilling					

Now you're going to take the words or phrases that you used the most frequently in each category. Ideally you want to take your top 3 or 4 in each column, so the ones with the most marks next to them are the ones you're looking at.

Write these into the new table and put them in order of importance, i.e. put the ones with the most marks at the top.

Real-life example:

DEALBREAKERS				FEELGOODS	
What made you start?		What made you leave?		What did you enjoy most?	
Offices were beautiful	1 1 1	Monotonous, not learning anything new	1 1 1	Trusted to do things my way and get on with it	1 1 1 1
Good money	1 1 1	Money	1 1 1	Organising, making things work efficiently	1 1 1 1
Work would be varied	1 1	Wanted to travel	1 1	Designing	1 1 1
		It was very lonely work	1 1	Excellent feedback and appreciation	1 1

31. Input your most frequently used words or phrases from the table in question 31 into the table below. You want the top three or four for each question. Write them in order of importance, i.e. put the words or phrases you used the most frequently at the top of each category.

DEALBREAKERS		FEELGOODS
What made you start?	What made you leave?	What did you enjoy most?

The first column tells you, in order of importance, what will motivate you to go and work at a company, or start a business, or register on a course. The second column tells you, in order or importance, what will make you leave if these factors come into play.

These two columns together give you your DEALBREAKERS, i.e. the things that will make you decide whether or not you will do it and continue to do it.

The third column tells you, in order of importance, what will make you feel happy and joyful in your work. I call these your FEELGOODS.

You can see from my own real life example that, if the working environment is beautiful, it's good money and the work is varied, I'll say yes. But if the work becomes monotonous, I'm not learning anything new, I'm offered better money elsewhere, I want to move geographical locations (to travel or whatever) and if I'm lonely, I'm likely to quit.

If I'm able to work autonomously, I get to organize things and make them work efficiently, I get to do some design work, and I get lots of excellent feedback and appreciation, then I feel happy in my work.

What this tells me is that I need to work in pretty surroundings, I need to be getting paid properly, I need to be kept interested with varied tasks and new things to learn, I need to be able to travel or move locations when I feel like it and I need to have interaction with people so that I don't get lonely. And I'm happiest when I get to decide when and how I work, I get to organize and make things efficient, and design with words and images, and get great feedback.

Notice that this does NOT give us the TYPE of work that's ideal for us, but HOW we need to go about doing whatever work we decide to do, so that we will stick at it, and we'll feel happy doing it.

So now it's your turn to really analyse the information in the last table and consider carefully what it tells you about yourself.

Write in the space below a few sentences about what factors need to be in place for you to decide to do something (column one)? What factors will make you decide to quit (column two)? And what needs to be happening for you to feel happy in your work (column three)?

LisaCherryBeaumont.com

STEP 4: YOUR ALCHEMIC FUSION

Welcome to Step 4 of Life Purpose Alchemy.

This is the bit where the magic happens. What you're going to do is combine the "ingredients" of all the first three steps, to create your own unique recipe.

It may be that what you come up with is already an existing "job" that someone else will employ you to do. Or it could be a totally unique business idea, or it could be a business that others are already doing and you'd like to do something similar.

There's no right or wrong way, just the one that feels good to you.

1. Go back to Step 1 and quickly read through your answers, to get them fresh in your mind.

2. Write down your answer from question 29 from Step 2.

3. Write out your results to Step 3 (copy from the table on page 29).

DEALBREAKERS		FEELGOODS	
What made you start?	What made you leave?	What did you enjoy most?	

LisaCherryBeaumont.com

You're doing really well! You know what you want your dream lifestyle to look like, you know roughly what you want to do for a living, you know what skills you have, and you now know what motivates you (your dealbreakers) and what feels really good to you (your feelgoods).

Using all this information, use the following two pages to free-write some ideas about what you could do to earn a living. Play with ideas, without restriction. Don't worry if it sounds crazy or too "way out" – put all your ideas down and don't limit or edit what you write. Use more paper if you need to.

 LisaCherryBeaumont.com

32. Go back over what you've written in the last couple of pages and underline or pick out what seems like something you'd love to do, even if you're not sure of the way forward just yet. Write it out below.

Now answer the following questions:

33. What is your new working job title? (You can always change this later, but give it a name for now). e.g. Dog Trainer, Vegan Italian Restaurant Owner, Wellbeing Motivational Speaker.

34. What will be unique about how you do what you're going to do? e.g. I will specialise in working with poodles. I will have an open kitchen so that customers can watch the chefs make fresh vegan pasta and dairy-free cheese. I will sing motivational songs during my speeches and encourage audience participation.

35. How will I be making the world a better place by doing this thing I want to do? e.g. Poodle owners will have better-behaved dogs which will help the owners and their dogs to be happier and less stressed. There will a place for vegans to eat Italian food and they will learn how to make egg-free pasta and dairy-free cheese. I will motivate my audience to take action on their own wellbeing, and help them to feel a sense of belonging while participating in the songs which will make them feel happier.

STEP 5: YOUR WHAT IFS

Welcome to Step 5 of Life Purpose Alchemy.

Wow! Now you've got a pretty clear idea of what you want to do for a living - great going! In the final step we'll be defining it further and creating the first steps to making it happen.

But before we come to that, we need to make sure that you're geared up with a mindset that will help you to be successful because, let's be honest, going for the work that's deep-down important to you can feel really scary, and so you'll probably start sabotaging yourself, throwing roadblocks into your own pathway, with all sorts of stories as to why you shouldn't be doing it.

Don't worry; I've got you. In this step we'll face the top ten fears that may stop you in your tracks; the most common ones that prevent people from going after their dream work.

Because we don't want you to have figured out what you want and then are too scared to go for it, this step will take your fears and turn them on their head into positives that will give you confidence and motivate you to move forward.

Again, don't skip this step, even if you're feeling confident right now, this work will stick in your mind and will pop up for you when you need it in the future.

36. WHAT IF IT'S CRAP?!

You have an idea/product/service that you're holding back with because you're worried it might be a bit, well, crap.

Maybe it's a business idea that you haven't explored properly or done anything with, or maybe you've started on it but you're not making the effort to get it finished, or maybe it's finished but you're not telling people about it.

Listen, it's absolutely normal to feel scared about this stuff, you're just trying to keep yourself "safe" but, as you know, sitting in your safe zone isn't going to get you a fabulous business. So what we're going to do is flip your thinking to help get you over that fear hump.

If you're drawn to create something - whatever it is - then you need to create it and put it out there and not let fear trip you up. If your heart's in it, then it isn't crap - it's the LAW, damnit! (I know you know this deep-down.)

Answer the following questions:

1. What is your idea/product/service?

2. Who is it for and how can it help them?

3. What are three of the best things about it?

4. What three things can people be certain of when they buy a product or service from, or work with, you?

Example:

1. I want to open my own poodle grooming parlour.

2. It's for people with show poodles who want them to look their absolute best.

3. I have my own show poodles so I know the challenges they face. I will stock the full range of coloured dyes and ribbons. It will be open 16 hours a day for 3 days prior to Crufts.

4. A precision grooming - I'm really good at getting that afro symmetrical. A happy poodle - I have a way with them and they love me. Reliability - I will always turn up to bookings on time and give my undivided attention.

37. WHAT IF SOMEONE STEALS MY IDEA?!

You have an idea/product/service that you're holding back with because you're worried that someone might steal your idea.

Here's what you need to remember:

+ NEWSFLASH! Unless you've invented time travel your idea probably isn't an original one. If it is, you may want to patent it. Otherwise, get used to the fact that there are others doing what you do, and that's a good thing.

+ There's room for everybody. You know your favourite clothing brand? Do you think they looked at the fact that there are millions of others making clothing and thought, "Well, hell, there isn't room for us!" No, they recognised that they have something different and unique to bring to the table. And so do you.

+ Only you can do EXACTLY what you do, the way that you do it. Only you has your voice, your way of doing things, and so you will attract those who resonate with that. Others doing what you do will have their own voice and their own way of doing things that attracts THEIR ideal clients. Not everyone is for everyone and that's a good thing.

+ If someone steals your actual work - for example you write a book or a course and they copy it - then it's reassuring that you can sue their pants off as long as it is copyrighted. And if it's not, be reassured that someone who is lazy and unoriginal enough to present someone else's work as their own will not get very far.

A fear of someone stealing your idea is NOT a reason to not bring your work into the world. There are several dictionaries, Vietnamese restaurants, drum teachers, ashtanga yoga practitioners, self-esteem online courses... Someone needs what only YOU can do the way that YOU do it, please don't deprive them of it, it's your duty to put it out there.

1 Write down the name of your favourite restaurant (or clothing brand, or another business you love if you're not into restaurants or clothes).

2 Write down three things you love about it that, for you, sets it apart from others doing the same thing.

3 Write down three things about your business (or your style of doing things, if you don't yet have a business) that sets it/you apart from others doing something similar.

Example:

1 Shoko Club & Restaurant (I love that place!!!)

2 The food is outstanding and always beautifully presented. They do an unbeatable lunchtime deal - it's an absolute no-brainer. I get to eat my lunch in gorgeous surroundings overlooking the beach with great music in the background.

3 I have a brilliant knack of being able to see the lessons and the positives in difficult situations. I can just be myself and not "professional" and so people can get to know, like and trust me very quickly. I've been studying happiness from every angle for years and years and so I know all the tricks.

       LisaCherryBeaumont.com

38. WHAT MAKES ME THINK I'M AN AUTHORITY?!

You have an idea/product/service that you're holding back with because you're thinking, "Well, who the heck died and made ME the authority?!"

You're wondering what makes "little old you" good enough to actually get PAID to do this thing. But here's the truth:

You do NOT have to be The World Class Leader in whatever-it-is in order to be "good enough", and here's why:

Who's the world's best women's shoe designer?

Maybe Christian Louboutin? Wow, those shoes are a work of art, and are highly coveted.

Now tell me how many women you know actually own some. Ummm errrr... one? Two. None? And even those that do own Louboutins only have one or two pairs. And that's because, cost aside and beautiful as they are, they're spectacularly unpractical and sometimes they're just not what we need.

NOW tell me: How many women do you know own shoes? I'll hazard a guess that every woman you know owns somewhere between four and 40 pairs of shoes.

And here's the crux: almost NONE of them are designed by the world's best women's shoe designer!

Are you getting my drift? In case you still haven't caught on:

Should everyone who's not Mark Knopfler resign themselves that they're never gonna get that solo in Sultans of Swing so they ought to pack it in and stop embarrassing themselves?

Should all restauranteurs who don't own The Wolseley lock up their roller shutter doors and go put their CV in at McDonalds?

Should all film directors who are not Steven Spielberg just stop fooling themselves that people might want to watch their films?

Hell, no! Can you imagine a world like that? There's room for ALL of us to be doing our thing. Scrap that, there's a NECESSITY for all of us to be doing our thing!

If you're good at something...

if others come to you when they have a question about it...

and if you're wildly passionate about it...

then you need to be doing it.

1. Write down the name of a musician/writer whose music/books have helped you in your life.

2. Go on the internet and find out about their upbringing/background before they were famous - Wikipedia is good for this. Or if they're not particularly famous write down what you know about their background. Find something about this person's background that is similar to your own, and write a sentence or two about it.

3. On a scale of 1 to 10, how grateful are you to this person for creating their music/books in spite of how scary it might have been for them?

4. Write down one thing that people naturally seem to ask you to help them with. (It doesn't have to be your work, it can be anything.)

5. On a scale of 1 to 10, how good do you feel when you've been able to help someone with something?

 LisaCherryBeaumont.com

Example:

1. Susan Jeffers with her books "Dare to Connect" and "Feel the fear & do it anyway".

2. She abandoned her studies the first time round, then studied psychology later in life, she wrote self-help books, and ran workshops.

3. 10.

4. How to feel happier.

5. Off the scale. But yes, 10.

39. WHAT IF I CHANGE MY MIND?!

You have an idea/product/service that you're holding back with because you're worried that, once you've done all the hard work, the honeymoon period will come to a screeching halt and you'll be stuck looking at something you no longer love, thinking it was a complete waste of time.

It's essential that you do what you're truly passionate about and that you enjoy it, and that, however you do it, you stay within the boundaries of your own personal values. If you do this, then it's NEVER going to have been a total waste of time. But there's something else that's very important that often gets missed and that is...

TAKING CARE OF YOUR WELLBEING.

One of the main reasons that business owners and employees suffer burn-out (and therefore jack it in, thinking they don't enjoy it anymore) is because they get so wrapped up in their work that they've forgotten to follow the basics of taking care of themselves.

It's SO easy to get borne along on a wave of entrepreneurial late-nights-at-the-laptop while your arse spreads from too little exercise and your brain fogs over from the overwhelming to-do list and lack of fresh vegetables in your take-aways. But you wouldn't let an employer insist you work 16 hours straight (or I hope not, anyway!) so don't do it to yourself or you'll suffer. Schedule in leisure time, down time, fun, proper meal times, exercise, and socialising - and stick to it no matter how essential it seems at the time to sit in a training webinar at 3am.

It's important that you're conscious of how you're taking care of yourself and you create some good habits that you can stick to.

Take a good look at your lifestyle as though you were looking at it through the eyes of a concerned health practitioner. Are you:

Drinking enough water?

Eating enough fruit & veg?

Getting enough sleep?

Taking enough breaks?

Getting outside enough?

Getting enough exercise?

Spending enough time with friends?

Being fulfilled spiritually?

Having enough fun?

Be totally honest with yourself here - which of these needs some attention? I want you to pick one or two of them, create a realistic goal for yourself, and stick to it.

Example:

I'm not being fulfilled spiritually so I have committed to a weekly tai chi class.

I'm not eating quite enough fruit & veg so I've committed to eating at least one piece of fruit at breakfast time every day.

40. WHAT IF I CAN'T MAINTAIN MOMENTUM?! (For business owners.)

You have an idea/product/service that you're holding back with because you're worried that after your initial burst of enthusiasm, you won't be able to keep up the momentum.

Whether you have a business yet or not, you know that, at some point you're going to need to get visible on social media.

But you're worried you'll attract a hoard of raving fans from your daily Periscopes, twice-daily Instagrams, your twice-a-week blog posts, your weekly newsletters, your 5-times-daily engagement in Facebook groups... *GASP!* and breath...

(and that's as well as doing that thing you went into business to do!)

... and then you'll find your enthusiasm for all this drops off and your potential clients will fall away and you'll be back to square one, sitting in your pyjamas looking at job ads.

What you're scared of is overwhelm, and boredom. You're scared you'll give yourself too much to do, and that you'll feel overfaced. And you're worried you'll get sick of it and not want to do it any more.

Start out as you mean to go on; be authentic with YOURSELF. Be honest and realistic about what you ENJOY doing and what you can do CONSISTENTLY, and then build it into your schedule.

If you hate making videos, don't make videos. If you love being motivational on Instagram, guess what you need to do more of! Only do what you love.

The trick is to make it ENJOYABLE, SUSTAINABLE & CONSISTENT.

Now, it's NOT a good idea to spread yourself thinly on social media - although it makes sense to have a presence over as many platforms as possible, it's better to create deep relationships on fewer platforms, than shallow relationships on loads of them - so keep that in mind. Social media experts recommend that we have a "marker" on each platform and, for the ones, we don't really use, have it pointing to the ones we use the most. (For example, on my Facebook page which I rarely use, I have pinned to the top, "Come and find us over at my group where all the action is!")

Start looking at some of the social media options that you may not have thought of using. You can find them by Googling "top ten social media platforms" to find out what's current.

I want you to investigate one other social media platform that you don't usually look at, and spend 20-30 minutes taking a look around, finding out how it works, and deciding if you'd like a presence on it, then write below whether you think you'll have a new love affair with any of them or if they had you running away like your pants were on fire!

Example:

I love the way that Facebook groups work and I enjoy being in them. I've investigated using LinkedIn groups and they don't feel right to me because everyone is so stiff and corporate.

 LisaCherryBeaumont.com

41. WHAT IF PEOPLE THINK IT'S NOT WORTH THE PRICE?! (For business owners.)

You have an idea/product/service that you're holding back with because you're worried that people will think it's not worth the price.

There are three main themes with this fear:

1 You're comparing your prices to what others are charging for a similar thing.

2 You're scared that others offer a product or service that is superior to yours.

3 You're scared that your ideal customer can't afford you.

You've got to put all that crap aside. It's irrelevant what others are doing and what they're charging for it. They're not you and their clients are not your clients. And no matter what you charge for what you do ($50 or $50,000), there'll ALWAYS be someone who gasps in horror and says they "can't afford it" and there'll always be those who eye you suspiciously wondering why you're so cheap!

You've heard "your vibe attracts your tribe"? When you're comfortable with the price you're charging for your "thing", you'll give off a positive energy and your people will naturally gravitate toward you.

If you charge a price that energetically feels too low to you, as well as ending up broke, you will start to feel reluctant about giving 100% to your customers because you won't feel like they're paying you enough, and that can cause resentment.

Conversely, If you charge a price that energetically feels too high to you, you will feel like a fraud, like you're ripping people off, like you're not providing enough value for the price you're charging, and you'll become nervous when discussing your prices with potential clients, for fear of them gasping in horror. And that negative vibe will show through and you'll scare people off.

It's nobody else's job to tell you what you should charge for your products and services. After all, you know how much money you want to earn, you know what experience you have - how much time and money you've spent and what you've been through to learn it all and what value you're providing - and therefore you know deep-down what you feel comfortable with charging.

Think of a product or service that you've bought fairly recently that was similarly priced to another similar product/service and write down why you chose that particular one.

Example:

Even though there were coffee machines at a similar and even cheaper price that were bigger and more robust-looking, I chose this particular one because it fits the space better in my kitchen and it just kind of "felt right"!

42. WHAT IF I'M IGNORED?! (For business owners.)

You have an idea/product/service that you're holding back with because you're worried that you'll put it out there and only get crickets/tumbleweed (i.e. nobody takes any notice).

What you need to understand here is that you are going to create (or already have created) a product or service that you KNOW is going to have a positive effect. You wouldn't be doing it, otherwise, would you?

What you're going to be creating (or have already created) is something that, even if you were a squillionaire and didn't need the money, you'd do it anyway because it's THAT important to you.

And because it's that important to you, you have to get over that fear that you'll be ignored. You WILL be ignored, by those who don't need what you do, you may even be ridiculed or patronised by those who simply don't get how important your work is (and we'll come to that but not in this moment). And that's OK, they're not your ideal client anyway.

Sometimes you WILL get crickets and tumbleweed. The important thing to keep reminding yourself is that your people are out there, and you've got to be visible for them to find you. If you hide away, they can't find you, and therefore you won't be able to help them.

What you must focus on is putting yourself out there with love and consistency - even when it feels like you're being ignored - and remember that people are watching, even though they're not necessarily engaging with you immediately.

Write about a product or service you bought either recently or in the past that you'd had your eye on for quite some time but you didn't mention it to anyone until after you'd bought it. What made you wait?

Example:

At the end of 2014 I read about a 12 week business course. It was a pretty big, scary (time and money) investment and I didn't buy it straight away; I had to be sure it was what I really needed. I slept on the idea, I read about it a few times. I slept on it some more and didn't mention it to anybody, and I didn't say anything to the course leader; she had no idea I might be interested! And then eventually my brain did the processing it needed to and I booked myself onto the course.

43. WHAT IF I GET NEGATIVE COMMENTS?! (For business owners.)

You have an idea/product/service that you're holding back with because you're worried that you'll get negative comments.

Have you ever noticed that, no matter what you do, you simply cannot please everyone? Of course you have. You open the window and someone complains their hands are cold, you shut it and someone else complains their hair's sweating.

Someone posts on Facebook or Twitter a controversial article and fights break out. If you've ever tried to voice your opinion on 9/11, breastfeeding or Muslims you'll know exactly what I'm talking about: human beings are largely a bunch of know-it-alls, hugely divided in our views on what is the "correct" way to live life, believing it's our duty to instruct others about what's right and wrong.

And most people are conditioned by our society into believing that, unless you've got a "proper job" then what you're doing must be worthless, it's pointless, it's all wrong, you're a rip-off, it's silly, you're wasting your time, it's just a hobby, blah blah blah...

So, when you come along with your business, whether you're talking about it in person, or you've written a blog post about it, or you're putting yourself out there on social media, or you're sticking posters up on local noticeboards... there's going to be somebody who doesn't agree with what you're doing and/or how you're going about it and they can't wait to tell you!

Occasionally, you may get a bit of useful "feedback" (that you didn't ask for) but, more often than not, the negative comments will be spiteful comments from people who are bored or jealous or don't understand what you're doing, or "well-meaning advice" from people who have got absolutely no idea what they're talking about.

So, if it's written criticism ignore it or delete it. If it's verbal criticism, thank them for their concern and either walk away or change the subject. NEVER give it your attention.

Caveat: In order to grow and improve your business you will want to request feedback from your customers, in which case, you can do this in a structured and helpful way. Reading hater-comments is NOT a structured and helpful way, in case you were wondering.

Imagine you're at a gathering at a friend's house and you meet a new person, and they ask you what you do. You excitedly explain your business or your business idea to them, and they pull a sad face and say,

"Oh, I don't think that's a good idea. I mean, you can't make a proper living out of it. I used to know someone who tried it. They told me it was too hard and, after spending loads of money on trying to get it off the ground, they failed and went back to a normal job."

What will your response be?

44. WHAT IF MY SALES TALK ANNOYS PEOPLE?! (For business owners.)

You have an idea/product/service that you're holding back with because you're worried that your sales posts will annoy your friends and family.

You already know that you need to be visible in order for people who need you to find you. You want to help (somebody or something) in some way and you're not helping anyone or anything if nobody can find you! You've got to put yourself out there.

But what if, while you're "putting yourself out there" you start to irritate your friends and family with your "sales talk"?

Those who care about you want you to do well. If they know you well, they understand why you're doing what you're doing, and want to support you. And if they don't care about you, know you well or want you to succeed then who cares if they walk away? Let them go!

Just as what YOU take in from other people is YOUR responsibility, other people are responsible for what they take in from you. So, if someone is annoying you, it's up to you set your own boundaries such as changing the subject if you're talking in person, or unfollowing their feed on social media. And the same applies if you're irritating someone else: it's up to THEM to do something about it; it's not your problem.

It's natural when you're on the path of personal growth (and being in business will provide you with more personal growth than you ever thought possible!) for some of the people you once connected with to fall away. It could be a permanent falling-away or a temporary one and either of those is OK.

Look out today, in person, on the TV, on a billboard or on social media, for someone talking about something you're not interested in. It could be an advert that you see a lot of, or it could be a friend talking (AGAIN) about something you couldn't care less about. And notice what you do. Write about it below.

Example:

A colleague whom I like and respect enormously has an advert running on Facebook at the moment. It's not for something I'm interested in buying. But I like her and support what she's doing. So I just scroll past it. No screaming rage, no bashing the unfriend button with fury, no drama at all.

45. WHAT IF I DON'T END UP FULFILLED?!

You have an idea/product/service that you're holding back with because you're worried that you won't end up feeling fulfilled.

When you start out in business or a new job there's the possibility that you'll eventually change your mind about it, and want to do something else. If you're a serial-business-starter (i.e. you've jumped from one business to another to another...) or a job-hopper you'll know what I mean. And, understandably, you want to avoid that frustration, as much as you can.

The reason you might begin to feel unfulfilled in your work is usually because you're "following the money" instead of your heart, i.e. instead of focusing on doing only what lights you up inside, you're focusing more on what will make you a good income. Now, that's not to say that doing what you love won't make you money. It's that if you chase the money, the fulfilment is unlikely to follow. Start with fulfilment and the money follows.

What happens when you "follow the money" is that you stop living and working in line with your own personal values. So, even if you ARE doing what lights you up, you're doing it in a WAY that isn't working for you. For example, if one of your personal values is to spend lots of quality time with your family, yet your work (no matter how much you love it) is taking too much of your time away from your family, you're going to feel unhappy. Start with knowing your personal values and ensure your work is built around them. (Your Dealbreakers & Feelgoods, Step 3.)

1 Think back to a hobby that you used to enjoy that you no longer participate in but would kind of like to start doing again. Did you used to go to dancing classes when you were younger? Horse-riding, painting, badminton, skating, photography..? What was yours?

2 Write down three things you loved about it.

3 Write down what you think your personal values are relating to these three things.

4 Write down the main reason that you stopped doing it.

5 Write down what you could have done to continue participating in this hobby.

Example:

1 I used to go to street dance classes when I lived in London.

2 It was a fun challenge to learn moves that were totally different to the types of moves I learnt in other dance classes. I enjoyed the togetherness of us all doing the same moves at the time time. It was great exercise which kept me fit and lifted my mood.

3 I like to learn new things that challenge my normal way of doing something. I like to feel a part of a community; all of us working together. I enjoy the feeling I get (physical and emotional) when I move my body.

4 The classes stopped and I never made the effort to find another class.

5 I could have contacted the school and asked if/when the classes would be restarting, or I could have asked around friends if they knew of a class.

STEP 6: YOUR UNIQUE PATHWAY

Welcome to Step 6 of Life Purpose Alchemy.

In this final step we'll really define your goal and create the first steps of your unique pathway to get you physically moving toward your dream work. Because that's what this is all about – getting you actually doing this thing!

Again, this step is creative but it's also very practical so put your focus and energy into it, as the more dedication you put into this, the more you'll get out of it.

You are doing this to create the first practical steps you need to take to go out into the world and make this thing happen; to make your dream become your reality.

46. Write down the working title of your purpose (question 33).

47. What I will be doing is: (question 32)

48. Whether directly or indirectly, who will you be helping with your work? (Examples: Newly married couples, divorced men, children who love to dance, students struggling with homework, homeless dogs...)

49. What problem(s) will you solve for them?

50. How specifically will you help them?

51. How will they benefit from your work?

52. How will you recognise that you're living your purpose? What will be happening to tell you that you're doing the job of your dreams? Write down as much detail as possible. Use the questions in the bullet points below as prompts.

What will you be doing?

Where might you be going?

How might you be feeling?

What will other people be doing?

LisaCherryBeaumont.com

53. When is it realistic to start getting paid to do this? (Don't over-think it, go with what feels good. Write down the date, month and year.)

54. Write your goal in the present tense into an outcome statement with a date on it.

It is the (date you wrote in question 53):

And I am getting paid to be a (title you gave your purpose in question 46):

55. What's telling you that you need to find your purpose right now?

56. The fact that you're not living your purpose at the moment, what impact is that having on you and others?

57. What's missing in your current job or career that you want?

58. What are you already doing that's contributing toward your life purpose?

59. What have you already tried to make steps toward your life purpose?

60. Of those things you tried:

which bits were successful? (If it was successful to begin with but then it broke down, what was it that contributed to the initial success, even if it was only temporary?)

what was the point at which it stopped? (If you tried it for a while and then stopped, what was the point at which it stopped? When it stopped working for you, what was all that about? What happened?)

61. What does that tell you? (If you're looking for a lesson that emerged from that, from things that you've tried, what's that telling you about yourself, about the process, about your actions?)

62. What are some of the obstacles that might get in the way of you living your purpose?

63. If you've encountered obstacles in the past when taking steps towards living your purpose, how did you manage to negotiate them?

Now you're in a position to think about how you can move forward. You're going to generate some options, and options are things that you <u>could</u> do, not necessarily things that you <u>will</u> do.

64. Make a list of things that you <u>could</u> do that would move you closer towards your life purpose. (Don't be self-critical, don't edit what you write, just let some ideas flow. Think about the lessons from things you've already tried – what does that prompt you into thinking you could do? Use the questions points below to generate some ideas.)

If you actually believed in yourself – fully – what could you do?

If you devoted yourself just to living your purpose what could you do?

If your resources were unlimited what could you do?

If you weren't scared of anything what could you do?

If others gave you space what could you do?

If you didn't have to live with the consequences, what could you do?

If you knew you couldn't fail, what could you do?

If you went to your boss or guru or a friend or your mum, what would they say you could do?

Think about the ideas that you put into practice in the past that went wrong. What could you have done that might have made a difference?

Read through the list you've just written, is there another option that springs to mind?

LisaCherryBeaumont.com

And what else? When you think you've exhausted it and you had to write down another couple, what would they be?

65. Look back at your answer to question 47, and make sure that the options you've written above would take you closer toward it. Sometimes when we start looking at options we generate lots of good ideas but they don't necessarily take us any closer to what we're trying to achieve. Cross off any that are not aligned to your purpose.

66. Look at your answers to question 64 and identify which are the most appropriate ones. Which are going to give you the best value, and are the ones you need to be doing?

67. Look at your list above and pick out one or two of these options that you're going to develop further.

68. Write down what specifically you need to do to bring about these options. (What are the little action steps you need to take to make them happen? If they seem overwhelming, break them down into their components.)

         LisaCherryBeaumont.com

69. Think about your obstacles to the above action steps. What will you need to do to make sure you negotiate them? (Think about what might stop you or get in your way and write down some simple steps around it.)

70. Does anyone else need to be involved, do you need to talk to them, and what do you need to tell them?

71. Look back at question 68. When is a realistic date to complete the actions that you've chosen to take?

72. Project yourself forward to a time when you've taken these actions from question 68. Imagine yourself in that position. What will be the benefits to you?

What will you be saying to yourself?

What will others be saying?

What will you be thinking?

What will you look like?

Where will you be going?

How will that feel?

73. On a scale of 0 – 10, how strong is your intention to carry out these actions? If 0 is I just won't bother and 10 is yep, that's something I'm committed to doing, I can see the benefits, I know the way forward, and that's what I'm going to do. You need to write down a number.

74. If it's not an 8, 9, or 10, what needs to happen to make it a 10?

75. Put these actions into your diary or calendar STRAIGHT AWAY! And be realistic with yourself about when you can get started. If you don't keep a diary or calendar write them into a notebook with dates against them. Keep in mind the completion date you wrote down in question 71.

76. The goal that you wrote in question 54, copy it into your diary or calendar on the date you identified in question 54. If you don't keep a diary or calendar, write it on a note with a date on, and stick it on your mirror or your computer.

77. The person/people you identified in question 70 that you need to talk to, have that conversation with them.

Really, really well done for completing this workbook – congratulations! Living your purpose is key to your happiness and you now have the awareness of what that is, and the first steps toward it.

If you still have some uncertainty, that's OK! Like I said at the beginning, it's fine to take your time to figure things out, and take a breather here and there. Often the answers to the questions come to you in the shower, or sitting in traffic. You can revisit your answers and the exercises as much as you like.

I'm Lisa Cherry Beaumont, The Life Purpose Alchemist, and I specialise in helping people to figure out their life purpose and get on with it. If you feel stuck or simply wish to talk about any aspect of your life purpose, your actions, or this workbook, drop me an email at lisa@lisacherrybeaumont.com and I'll be incredibly happy to hear from you.

If you'd like to connect with me on social media, I'd love that! Come over to my website LisaCherryBeaumont.com where you'll find the links.

www.ingramcontent.com/pod-product-compliance
Lightning Source LLC
Chambersburg PA
CBHW060419190526
45169CB00002B/972